Animal Hugs

A Waverley Story Book for Children

Written by Amanda Stanford
Illustrated by Jenny Moodie

The Reworkd Press
Charlotte, 2014

For wee Evie

Small hugs under ground.

Big hugs
in the ocean
sound

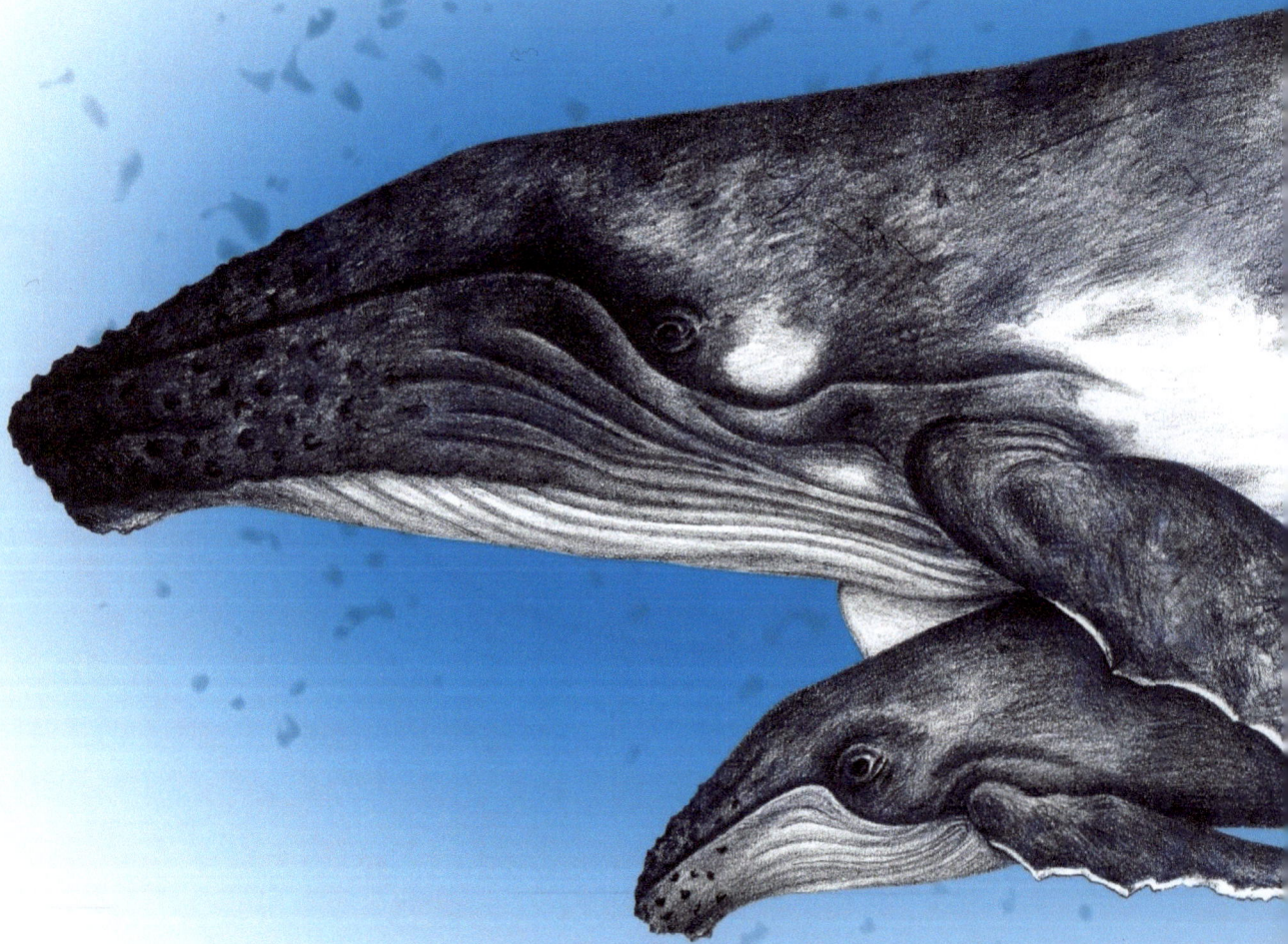

Mommy and
me up a tree

Soaring high like a buzzing bee.

A furry forest hug

A silent,
slithering
squeeze.

Dark, wet nose or ticky whisker sneeze

Snuggle close when you feel blue, hugs for me and hugs for you.

About the author:

Dr. Amanda Stanford earned her PhD in English Creative Writing from the University of Edinburgh. She has taught writing and English classes in the USA, Mexico, Japan, and Egypt. She also writes historical fiction under the pen name A M Montes de Oca.

About the illustrator:

Jenny Moodie is a self taught artist/illustrator, who has been drawing since she could hold a pencil. Jenny has a degree in multi-disciplinary design from Edinburgh Napier University. She currently splits her time creating artworks and wire jewellery to sell at local fairs and exhibitions and works in the events design and production industry. She creates her artworks using a simple graphite pencil and colours them with digital overlays.

www.ingramcontent.com/pod-product-compliance
Lightning Source LLC
Chambersburg PA
CBHW040020050426
42452CB00002B/62